My View from the Street

Pam Kumpe

Copyright © 2016 Pam Kumpe

THE HOLY BIBLE, NEW INTERNATIONAL VERSION®, NIV® Copyright © 1973, 1978, 1984, 2011 by Biblica, Inc.® Used by permission. All rights reserved worldwide.

All rights reserved. No part of this publication may be reproduced, distributed, or transmitted in any form or by any means, or stored in a database or retrieval system, without the prior written permission of the publisher.

Photos by Cindy Ross & Pam Kumpe

ISBN: 978-0692809273

DEDICATION

To my mom
who once cared for two little neighbor girls,
and taught me how kindness reaches across the fence row,
by using a little shampoo and a whole lot of love.

To Olivia West whose heart is filled with kindness.
Never lose your love for others.

Pam Kumpe

DISCLAIMER

On some occasions names, businesses, places, events,
and incidents were renamed to protect privacy.

All pictures are of my journey serving on the streets in Texarkana, Dallas, and even in Houston.
The photo beside each story is not necessarily the person or persons in that story.
The images depict a sampling of precious people God has allowed me to love and meet along the way.

Pam Kumpe

God is our refuge and strength,
an ever-present help in trouble.
Psalm 46:1 NIV

Blocked in a Parking Lot

On that weekend, I had one hygiene bag left in my car after Church Under the Bridge. I'd already handed out several to my homeless friends, thrilled to have dozens of the bags donated to me by a dear friend.

After buying a couple of my homeless friends some shoes too, I was leaving a parking lot near the library in Texarkana when I saw a stranger.

I saw Johnny, not that I knew his name yet, but he stood with two other homeless friends who had their hygiene bags from earlier. They walked along the sidewalk next to the parking lot, and I hopped out and gave Johnny my last bag, which was packed with goodies.

He stepped back a few steps as I ran up to him, and my other two friends moved on down the road, and the new friend asked, "Who are you?" He took a look into the bag, grinning. "I sure needed some toothpaste."

I patted his arm, "I'm God's little servant." I laughed, looking at myself. "Wait, I'm not so little." He glanced at me, and then laughed a bellow along with a giggle. We chatted, talked, and he shared some of his life story with me.

I then asked if I might pray with him.

"Sure. Please do."

After my saying amen, I hugged him as he clutched his bag, and I turned to leave. He tapped me on the shoulder, giving me his insight. "No one has ever jumped from their car, left it running, and blocked traffic in a parking lot just to talk to me."

I laughed again, looked at my idling car, and nodded. "Yeah, next time I might need to park my car in a spot. It seems I've blocked the driveway. That lady can't get by."

I hurried to the car behind mine, apologizing to the driver whose window was down. "Sorry, I didn't mean to cause a problem. I get caught up in things."

"I started to honk for you to come back, but when I noticed you were praying for that man, I knew I should pray for him, too."

Tears welled up in my eyes. "Oh, thank you so much."

Back in my car, I thought about how prayer warriors can find themselves blocked in driveways so they will pray. And how divine appointments unfold exactly as God would have them.

The meeting became a "where two or three are gathered in God's name" moment for me, and somehow I expect my new friend, Johnny, won't forget the parking lot prayer anytime soon either. Or the lady parked behind me waiting for me to move my car.

Pam Kumpe

Blank Pages Filled with Faces

Your story is being written on the blank page of today. And it could become a song for your heart, but sometimes a song can sound like a broken whistle when sorrow creeps inside of the moment. This is when singing in tune can be hard, and that's when you need a friend to comfort you, to hold you.

Friends can sing a song back to you when you have forgotten the words. So when I heard the news of a homeless friend being found unresponsive at the camps, my heart was broken. Losing a friend, or a family member, or anyone, should grip our hearts. It does mine. And unexpected goodbyes are never easy for me.

So I ponder the goodbyes of several friends over time. One person I will remember is Skip. His smile could part the Red Sea. His joy captured hearts. I remember Harley's sly grin. I remember his wife, Julie, and her giggle. I remember Bill's bent body, and how he slumped, and the way he rubbed his chin. I remember Paul's quiet voice, and Jeff's blue eyes.

I see others in my mind, those who come and go, like Montana Bones, the musician. Like David who rode his bike in the rain. Like Jimmy whose lanky stance towers over us. Like the young man whose last words to me before hitting the road again were, "You're pretty nice for an old lady."

I think of those who huddle at The Bridge. Of those who sit in the folding chairs. Of those who capture every part of the preaching on Saturday mornings for church service. Of those who waddle in, and those who stumble out. Of those who purpose to be there, and of those who are hungry. Not just for breakfast, but for the Word of God.

I think of those who wave to me when I arrive. Of those who make their way to me for a hug. Of those with whom I have prayed. Of those who linger at my car for blankets, for gloves, or even for a stuffed animal. Or for bug spray. Or to talk. To laugh.

Every one of them writes a story on my heart—for they are friends. And of course, my prayer is they serve Christ, and hear His call to their own heart. And I pray they search for hope, receiving mercy and grace from Christ, too.

Many are broken. Or sad. Some are hopeful. Some are lost. Some are filled with joy.

All of my friends make my heart sing, although sometimes my song is filled with loss when someone dies before I expect to say goodbye.

Either way, those relationships write lyrics on my life, even if sometimes the pain of the chorus is too much. Especially when a body is discovered beside a tent.

Then I'm reminded that joy comes in the morning, that Christ is my comfort on those terrible, no-good, very bad days, too. That my joy is found in Him.

I remind myself how grateful I am that the Gospel goes out from under The Bridge, no matter if it's freezing, no matter if it's raining, or even if the humidity is so thick water drips from the air. Pastor

Cody Howard has a love for others, and pours grace into lives, but he does not forsake the Gospel of Jesus Christ—Christ is the reason we gather in the first place.

So in those moments of loss, I pray for 'new music' like a breath of fresh air, so that I may keep on singing. And I pray for a 'new story' for the day, and also I pray the Lord compels me to return again and again to the streets to love on a homeless friend, or to serve in the recovery center, or to volunteer at the prison—because salvation from Jesus Christ is too important not to tell others. It is a matter of life and death—for the soul!

Breezing Down the Road

One weekend, I headed to Houston for a Christian concert with a friend, a weekend get-out-of-town escape. I also wanted to find a homeless friend I met once while taking part in Church in the Park with the homeless, a time when we passed out Bibles to those who wanted one.

The man I'd met that year grabbed my heart especially after I asked his name, because he said, "I'm That Guy, and in a few days, when you go home, you'll try to remember my name. You'll say, That Guy. You won't remember me. Or my name."

That hurt so much when he said that to me, and I think of his words often—and they sting every time. He's probably right in some respects, because there's no telling how many others I've forgotten along the way. But one great thing happened that day, his words caused me to never forget his name! It's Brian, and I even dedicated my book, *My View from The Bridge* to him, so I will always remember him.

So on the weekend I drove back to Houston, I searched for Brian, driving to the places where some meet, linger, and hang out. I carried a care package with me in hopes of finding him, in hopes of letting him know I hadn't forgotten him.

On Sunday of the trip, I was still searching for him, and realized I had about five hours left to find my friend before heading home.

For, you see, I had brought a new blanket stitched by a pair of small hands by a young lady who never thought she'd create such a beautiful item. I also had a new Bible for Brian, and a backpack filled with hygiene items, and a giant bag of candy, along with socks and some cash.

I passed the park one more time, even though it was closed due to construction, and I circled The Bridges where the homeless gather, only to drive near a parked police car beside the park. I turned around, I stopped again, and I circled back the other way.

Two hours later, yes two, I decided to pray. Time was getting away, and I should have opted for this at the beginning of my journey, but sometimes I go out on my own, and forget to let God lead me. So I parked my car, and my friend Cindy and I prayed for the Lord to show us who to deliver the items to, since I couldn't find Brian. I'd run into dozens of homeless—all in desperate need. One man sat in the median holding a sign while pigeons landed on the concrete around him.

But I wanted a clear picture of the person God wanted me to give my gift to, and so I drove back down the side streets, and I saw a man who stood like a statue.

I drove back beside the man sitting with the pigeons and I saw a man under The Bridge reading the newspaper. Another stared off into space across the way. And a group huddled together in the cold. But I had no clear picture of who to surprise with the gifts.

After four million trips (it felt like that) up and down and around the park and bridges, I saw a lone man with his head in his hands, and he was perched on a concrete wall. He sat alone.

My police officer friend had finally moved on down the road, which meant I could connect with my homeless friend without interruption.

I stopped my car and jumped from the seat, running to him. And I think he was afraid of me—at first, until I told him I prayed for the person to love on for Jesus.

Yes. I'd met a new friend. His name is Louie, and I'll always remember him, too.

His smile. His gait. His joy became plastered in my memory. I will also remember how he held the brown and turquoise blanket, and how he gave me a toothless grin as I waved goodbye.

I'm sure he found the money later, and I'm sure he loved chocolate, too. At least, I hope so. But either way, I can still picture how he searched the bag like opening a present at Christmas.

Don't you love how God can take our detours, our distractions, and divinely send us to a lonely heart? On my outing, it's a wonder the police officer didn't run my plates that day since I drove by him at least ten times!

Oh wait, he may have run them, and figured I was harmless. Or figured I was blonde and simply lost. But what I love more is that after we prayed, we found Louie—and he was the first homeless man I'd noticed when I rounded the park earlier in the day!

No, I didn't find Brian, but I did find Louie, which is a reminder that all around us are people like Brian and Louie—alone, in need of a friend, in need of compassion and in need of grace.

May you find someone to show kindness to today, and pray about who it might be—so you don't circle the same block again and again, like I did!

My View From the Street

Eggs for You

    A friend drove to Church Under the Bridge in hopes of sharing her fresh eggs with some of my homeless friends. After walking around, she didn't deliver them, as she wasn't sure who to pass them to or who needed them. She had hoped to find me, but I wasn't even there on that Saturday since I was speaking at a women's brunch.
    On that day, around noon, the meeting ended, and I carried my Bible and some other items with me, and walked right past my friend who was now eating lunch at the very restaurant where I had spoken in one of the conference rooms.
    My friend saw me through the window as I left the building, and she tapped on the window, mouthing to me. Reading her lips came easy, but after she said something about eggs, I had to go inside to figure out what eggs, and whose eggs.
    Back inside at her table, with my arms still loaded, she told me she didn't know or see who to give the eggs to earlier in the morning, so she put them in her car.
    She rushed to her car, while I protected her plate of food, and she brought the cartons to me to pass out to my friends. We laughed at our running into each other, and as far as I can remember I have never once run into her anywhere prior to that day.
    Now if you are one who believes God directs our steps, you'll agree with me when I tell you God sent my friend to the restaurant where I was, on purpose. My friend had eggs. And I could get them to the recipients, to precious friends who would love to have fresh eggs.
    When the morning began, I thought my purpose was to lift and encourage business women in Texarkana, but God was up to something better. He was ordering my steps to put eggs inside of my car so I could drive to the homeless camps with them.
    Dropping the eggs off came with a hug from a homeless friend, who smiled like a toddler who had a secret. One that says, God cares about eggs, too.

Bus Stop and Bold Steps

It all came together at a bench at a bus stop. Let me set the scene.

In Atlanta, Texas, a friend slipped away from a mission he was staying at, disappearing and going back to the street for a weekend of whatever.

In New Boston, Texas, a friend gave me a pair of 6 1/2 women's gold flats shoes. So I carried them in my car for Church Under the Bridge and once there, I didn't give them much thought. I had another delivery or two to make to some friends, not counting the fact that I was focused on attending the service and ready to fellowship with everyone.

Back in the car after service, I stopped off at God's Closet to leave some clothes, as I remembered the giant box in my trunk filled with great items. I made those stops and came across the box with the shoes, and drove around the downtown area praying, "Lord, you have someone in mind for these. Let me find her."

The box now sat in the front seat of my car and I lifted the lid to look at the petite shoes. Some people have the tiniest feet, but not me. My toes would take up most of those shoes, not counting that I have the flattest feet, much like a duck.

I drove by the library, and my car took me to a parking spot at the park where I found myself running like Forest Gump across the grass to a couple I know who attend The Bridge services. They sat on a bench waiting for the bus, their eyes glued on me with a curious stare as if they were watching that scene in the movie where the braces fall from Forest's legs, where he's free to run without restraints. And then keeps running for his life!

I rushed to Bonnie, "What size shoe do you wear?"

She grinned. "Why?"

"I might have your shoes."

She smiled and looked at her feet. "I have these tennis shoes. I'm fine."

"But I might have your glass slippers."

That's when the movie scene flipped in my mind from *Forest Gump* to *Cinderella* and I realized I was now mixing up my scenes. Actually, this was a real life God moment where the sovereign hand of the Lord brought me and Bonnie together—for such a time that we could be friends and find encouragement.

Now Bonnie shook her head saying she was good, but I ran up the hill to my car anyway, where I retrieved the sack with the shoes. Returning, I plopped down on the bench with her and looked inside the sack, and found some new socks and tossed them to the man who sat with her.

I then handed Bonnie the shoes. She lifted the lid, and hugged me. It was like she was being invited to the "Ball" and had the glass slippers. She told me, "Sometimes life gets heavy. Walking strong with God is hard."

So now you're asking, "What does this have to do with the man who left the mission?" Well, my pastor from The Bridge, Cody Howard, drove up next to my car on the hill, and from the passenger seat, Wingnut jumped out. Yes, you guessed it, Pastor Cody drove right past our little friend and gave him a ride, and now they were at the park with us.

He embraced Bonnie, wrapping both of his arms around her, while hugging my arm with the one draped on her back. In the next few seconds, I would pray with Bonnie, with her friend on the bench, and with Wingnut who was so excited to see all of us!

So yes, the shoes were a perfect fit! And yes, my friend who left the mission showed up just in time for prayer at a bus stop, just in time for hugs, laughter, and being with friends.

So here's my advice: No need to run from God. Just sit. Wait for Him to speak. Listen to His love letter of hope. Wear the Gospel shoes He slips onto your feet, because they'll always be the perfect fit.

Pending Toddler Trouble

One Saturday, I pulled up to a rather bustling intersection, a one-way street with several lanes filled with cars zooming faster than the speed limit. Well, most of them.

Across the street on the opposite corner, a toddler who was no more than two years old, darted from the alley—alone. He jogged ahead like a rock shot from a slingshot, and he raced for the street, twirling, his arms flapping like he'd turned into an airplane. He circled the parking lot like a Hot Wheels car without a track, like a propeller plane planning a lift off.

My mothering instincts, although I only have a few, kicked in because this little boy was a mere 30 or so feet from certain injury or even death—if he ran into the traffic.

I watched, frozen in my seat, with my foot on the brake, waiting for the cars to clear enough so I could dart across the road in my own little blue race car. It's not really a race car, it's just a Chevy.

Finally, I could get across, and I pressed the gas pedal, flying to the parking lot near the boy, and I parked between the highway and this precious little one.

I couldn't leave without knowing someone was looking out for him, and that he was going to be safe, and in someone's care. So I leapt from my car, and flapped my arms like an airplane, too.

And from one end of the street, a man emerged; a running, arms-waving person who obviously loved this little boy. Who could nearly fly, too!

It would seem that down the alley from behind a fence the boy had slipped through the gate, and now a woman charged toward the boy, her arms railing, and her words calling to him.

The youngster danced to the woman, happy to jump into her arms, his world of safety now back on track. We had a safe landing, and he had no idea just how close his life came to being filled with injury, tears, or worse.

The man would join them, and they would disappear behind the fence, but not before he waved to me, a thank-you-for-stopping wave.

My heartbeat slowed, and my breathing returned to normal, and I came in for a safe landing, too. Goodness, I wonder how many times we run from God, or how many times He's called to me, or to you; only for our pursuit of selfishness to put us in the path of oncoming disaster. Or do we run aimlessly ahead without seeing the danger?

I'm reminded of the verses in 1 Thessalonians 5: 9-10, "God has not destined you for wrath, but to obtain salvation through our Lord Jesus Christ, who died for you so that whether you wake or sleep you will live with him."

Christ came to give us life. To set us free from the path of certain death. When I saw that toddler it reminded me of the times I ran from God, and the best news of all is that He is there to lift me, to hold me, to call me to righteous living—with His tender but intense love. With His forgiveness. With His saving arms! He is the Rescuer!

Hungry in the Dark

Most of my friends (most of you) aren't usually sitting on curbs or wandering along the roads alone at 6 p.m. in the evening. When I saw Brenda sitting with her legs curled on the ground next to a building, I had to see her. She is one of my friends from The Bridge, and I wanted to visit with her for a minute—to let her know God loves her and sees her.

This happened right after I said to my friend Cindy, who was riding with me, "Too bad you have to be somewhere, I'm hungry."

Then it's like the Lord spoke to my selfishness, and instead had me stop the car only to discover Brenda was hungry, too. I drove to a fast food restaurant, zipped through the drive-thru and purchased the meal exactly as I would order, after telling Brenda to wait.

On a side note: The girl in the window was also a friend of mine, one of my girls who graduated from recovery/rehab nearly two years ago, and she remembered me from our church services. She's married, doing great, and serving God, so that moment was an extra bonus.

Now when I pulled my car into the empty parking lot, Brenda's grin lit up the sky. She was saying thank you for the meal before I handed it to her. And she tore into the sack, biting into the hot, gooey, cheeseburger loaded with onions.

Her gratefulness and her smile broke my heart, and being her friend blesses me beyond measure. I know that God in His sovereignty brought our paths together exactly as needed, and even now I weep and smile at such encounters. They bring me such joy in seeing God guide my steps, even when I'm not paying attention.

When I left Brenda, I wept and tried to steer my car back onto the street, and Cindy lectured me, asking me to wipe my eyes, to watch where I was going, to pay attention.

I have to say it's in those moments when I see God's beauty, that I am ever so grateful. There's nothing good in me, and everything beautiful is of Him. So keep watch. You never know when you'll run into a friend who may feel alone, who needs a friend, or maybe he or she just needs a hot meal. Besides, you will never regret showing kindness for the Lord ... never.

I love how Romans 2:4 tells us, "God's kindness is meant to lead us to repentance." Yes, God knows everything about us. He knows exactly how many breaths we will breathe. And He'll sit with us when we feel all alone on the road or even if we're "alone" sitting on our sofa—for He's food for the soul.

He's love for our heart!

When a Poem Flies

After Church Under the Bridge, I strolled down the trail to my car with my Bible in hand, and a crazy two hours would unfold as I searched for something I'd lost. And yet, in my missed steps and forgetfulness, God would reveal how He redirects my moves and how I can give Him glory along the way.

After service, I handed out water and Gatorade from my trunk on Broad Street, along with some batteries, bug spray, a new pair of tennis shoes, and some razors.

I'd placed my Bible on the top of my car while loving on my friends, chatting, laughing, and meeting some needs. And my once-homeless friend, David, needed a ride home, not able to ride his bike due to his health. He had taken the bus to town, but I was going to run him to his apartment a few miles away.

So I drove off, rounded the hill, and started to turn the corner, and a couple of friends walked close to my car, flagging me down. I pulled over, and one of them handed me my Bible because I'd left it on top of my car.

After dropping David off, I remembered that in the front of my Bible was a 2-inch note with a poem my twin sister wrote. It's dated 8/22/2009, and I checked the pages of my Bible, and the poem was gone. It must have flown out when my Bible was riding on top of the car.

I headed back to The Bridge and walked every inch of the grassy area and the ditches. All down Broad Street. And back. More than six times. Up and back. And all around.

Several of my homeless friends helped me as they wandered by, one by one. Five all together. We touched every piece of trash on the side of the road. But, no poem. Finally, an hour passes, and I'm dripping wet, sad at my loss. Sweaty with sorrow.

Then Tracy rides up on his bike and we chat about his children and his grand kids. I wish him a Happy Father's Day (since it's the next day), and he wipes tears from his face. We hug and pray and weep. We laugh and talk and weep some more. And I ended up giving him my last 24-pack of water, and I decided to look once more for the poem, and Tracey helped me.

I would find scraps and scraps of paper, but still no poem. Then I picked up a brown, wrinkled piece of paper, a page from a Bible. The words were from Hebrews and reminded me that God is my God.

And I'm his. He is my Savior! And He's written a poem of hope on my heart—for sure!

Once again, I saw the sovereign hand of Christ at work when He allowed me a most special time with Tracey and the others who live in camps. My loss became such a gain.

Leaving Texarkana, I had this revelation when I glanced at my Bible in the seat. Now, you won't believe it, but I have two brown Bibles and the poem was in the front of my OTHER brown Bible on my desk at home. The poem was safe at my house!!!

Yes, I can be a tad absentminded, but oh, I didn't mind the memories made that morning during my chaos. By thinking I'd lost something, I instead found my friends along the side of the road who made my day complete. I also picked up the scriptures from the dirt that encouraged my heart, and I also prayed with a dear friend.

For me, searching in the tall grass and weeds became a walk of pure glory as I touched dozens of pieces of trash, and I love that no detour I take is ever wasted by God. He is certainly my God, and He's not only the author of my heart, He's more like a poet who writes poems of joy in my day—in spite of my chaotic journey, in spite of where I leave my Bible.

And He lets me wish a lonely daddy "Happy Father's Day" only because I thought I'd lost a poem on the side of the road. Because He's that kind of God!

Arrested at Church

One weekend at The Bridge, the police arrested a friend of mine during our service. I share this with you because I want you to know that ministry is hard. Very hard. And very glorious!

As a pastor, Cody makes extremely difficult decisions. He's serious about his ministry and serious about fighting for the God-fueled joy of his people that Paul spoke of in Philippians 1:25, "I will remain and continue with you all, for your progress and joy in the faith."

My friend wasn't led away quietly, but rather she was handcuffed on the ground right in front of the congregation. The two Texarkana police officers were extremely gentle, kind and patient with her though, which comforted me.

I don't think they wanted to arrest her any more than Pastor Cody wanted to make the initial call, but he decided that she posed a danger to his people. After the arrest, one officer shared with Cody that she had been arrested earlier in the week so there was a good chance that she could now receive some psychiatric help.

So was this the right call? Was this decision made out of love for her? Was this decision made out of love for the rest of Pastor Cody's congregation? He thinks so, and I think so, but it doesn't mean the situation was without struggle.

While on the phone with 911 that's all he could think of, *Is this the path of wisdom and love for our mentally troubled friend?*

I'd learn that Cody felt sick to his stomach, but at the same time it seemed half of his people were looking at him with an, "Are you going to protect us?" expression on their face.

At The Bridge we have the most peculiar group of people on the planet. Seriously, Cody will tell you his congregation is weird, abnormal, alien – and he loves it.

They are trolls under a bridge that God has redeemed for His own glory, and oh, how they glorify Him!

In an extremely embarrassing and undignified situation, several of us prayed and pleaded with our troubled friend, and were very publicly threatened with bodily harm and cursed at, but we used words of compassion and love for this precious soul made in the image of our God.

You may ask why care? So I'll simply say, "She's our friend. She's family."

So yes, Pastor Cody must make decisions that are hardly ever easy, or cut and dry, but God, in His infinite grace and mercy has fashioned the body of Christ to work as a well-oiled machine, with each part supporting the other.

And when it works this way it churns out great glory to our King!

Even during and after such a traumatic event, we were able to keep our eyes set on the beauty of God, because it radiated through those who were silently sitting, silently praying, silently content with whatever suffering there was to endure, because we were at home with each other in the presence of our God.

So if you're inclined to pray, lift up my friend who got arrested or better yet, the entire congregation, and pray for Pastor Cody. God has placed him as a shepherd over the homeless community, and lives are glorifying Christ—and that, my friend, is beautiful even on days when the police come and when a friend gets handcuffed.

Popsicles for Pops!

I stopped my car at the intersection in downtown Texarkana, checking for traffic at the four-way stop. I pulled between the old buildings, the empty ones, the restored ones, the ones with no business inside, the ones made into lofts, the brick, and the frame.

I moved my car down a history-laced street where many lives have walked ... and then I saw ... I saw him. He leaned on the side of a tethered and worn brick wall, next to an empty spot where a building once sat. The man with the fuzzy hair sticking out like wire, waved at me as I rolled by, and he gave me a sly grin, a near wink, a look of recognition. I was sure he recognized me, but I didn't know him.

I made a right at the next corner and circled the block since I was passing out sacks of canned goods to homeless friends, or anyone I felt the Lord sending me to, and I wanted to stop for this man.

Back at the stop sign, the one north of the intersection, I headed down the same street again. I scanned the street, hoping to see the man who glanced at me only minutes before from the curb.

His eyes had seemed familiar; they held a glint of hope. His grin seemed familiar, too. And his gaze had pierced my being, stirring me. Who was this man?

I rolled my driver's side window down ready to call to him, but he was gone. His body no longer stood in the spot. No longer leaned on the wall.

I hurried in my little blue car to the next street, and turned. He was not there. I turned around, and went up and down those few blocks for more than 30 minutes. I never ... not once saw him.

I rolled to a stop at the last four-way intersection before leaving the area, my head twisting to the left and to the right in hopes of finding the man with the eyes.

Kablam!

A boom on the hood of my car brought me back to my senses and a tall lanky man, yes, the one from the wall, peered at me through the windshield. He now leaned forward on my car with both hands, and his blue eyes and his smile were like a green light of success.

He bounded to my opened window, bent down (he was like 6 feet tall or more), and spoke, "Miss Pam, you're sitting in the middle of the road and you don't have a stop sign."

"I'm so used to stopping. I thought I had a stop sign. I was looking for you."

"Well, I'm right here." He grinned and tapped my shoulder. "You're a funny lady."

My divine moment with this man came with my stopping in the wrong spot that turned out to be the right one. And I would learn this man was someone I gave a Popsicle to many years ago at a picnic for the homeless, and he remembered me, and my blue car.

He told me, "You laughed with me like a kid back then and you didn't mind sharing your Popsicles with me. You even let me pick the color I wanted. You even let me have extra."

I asked him, "So what's your name?"

"It's ... it's ... just call me Pops."

I laughed, "I will do just that. So keep watch, I think it's time for me to bring some more Popsicles."

"Thank you, and bring your laughter when you come. I need to be around those who see the good when the good is hard to see."

I giggled, "I will." I wiped a tear. "God bless you, Pops."

He walked back to the front of my car, tapped it with his hand, giving me the smile that touched deep inside my soul.

A honk from behind me would bring me back to the fact I was sitting in the middle of the road without a stop sign, and the car behind me wanted me to move.

I glanced over my shoulder at the pickup behind me, to only look right back and once again, the tall man with the eyes had disappeared from my sight.

This little "life intersection meeting" gave me hope, and reminded me how God can be glorified even in small things like passing out Popsicles on a hot day. It also reminded me that God remembers us when we think we're leaning on an empty wall of worry or doubt.

He will stop for us, talk with us, and remind us we are His. He will also remind us to keep on, keeping on, and He brings us His smile of love, always, even if it comes with honking. He saves us from the wrath of sin, and saves us to live in victory—to look for the broken, to shine our lights, to make a difference!

From Nose Hair to New Birth

Did you know that walking into the hospital to see someone's new baby can seem like going through gates at a prison? First, let me tell you that it was around 10 o'clock at night when I opted for this journey.

One of our couples from Church Under the Bridge had their second baby, a little boy. They are also the first couple to marry under The Bridge a few years ago. Since I was out of town most of the day, I was unable to be at the hospital when the baby was born, thus the late-night excursion.

By the time evening rolled around and the day's events concluded, I decided on a whim to go to the nursery and take a peek at the new little precious baby boy.

I first drove into the not-so-lit parking lot and couldn't decide on a parking spot where I felt safe, but I have good news for you. If you'll pull through emergency, zip around the hospital parking lot at least five times, the security truck will begin to follow you.

I finally parked, safe and secure and in the view of the security truck driver, and hurried through the emergency doors to scurry down the hallway. Just as I turned left, then right, I was met with closed doors, doors that were locked.

On the wall, there's a camera and you must speak into the tiny contraption by identifying yourself and your purpose for being there. I spoke louder than I should, faster than I meant, and had to repeat myself to the secret person whose voice jumped from the little box.

Tada! She approved my entry, and I flew down the long hallway to the elevators.

On the third floor, I stepped to the nursery where darkness lurked, and peered through the glass. There were no babies inside the room, but a paper on the window read: the babies are with their mothers.

I would soon discover this was not true, but I spun around anyway, and headed to the next closed set of doors. I found another tiny camera box, and I'm sure that my nose hairs were on full display to anyone who watched on the other end.

Repeating my purpose, my plan, and my desire, and after several announcements to the wall with my face only inches from the box—the approval rang out of the tiny contraption. I could now go through the doors to see the mother of the new baby.

Inside the room, I woke up my friend, slapped her leg, and congratulated her. She was quick to remind me that she had just had a C-section that morning and was quite sore. *Oops!* My rambunctious ways tend to leak over even late at night.

She was however, still thrilled for the company, but the baby was NOT in her room.

I'd learn he was in the second nursery and my mommy friend gave me directions to see him.

At the glass barrier, I could see two little cradle/carrier beds, and they were on the other side of the nursery room. The four nurses ignored my repeated taps, and glares, so I sighed with sadness and slumped off to the elevator.

As the doors closed, the daddy and his toddler daughter, and other family members for Jeremiah, the new baby, walked past me. I stuck my arm between the elevator door, and found myself back at the nursery where the daddy used his powers to have the little new life rolled to the window for my viewing.

So by the time the night concluded, I'd seized the moment, called out to everyone whom I could, and eventually saw the most precious little baby boy ever.

And so I must ask, do you seize your moments with God? Do you call out to Him? Or do you retreat to the elevator of life?

I'm reminded that this is the day the Lord has made, and He's the life giver. So look for His hand, He's the indescribable—all-loving Savior who is with you even when you stumble around in the dark.

Or when you can't seem to find a place to park! Or when you can't find the baby you've come to see! One gaze at the beauty of a new life is enough to shout with joy, even if your nose hairs are on full display on the camera at a hospital, too!

Bedding Blues

Seeing him during street ministry outings during the week allowed our friendship to grow, as well as seeing him at the services. This journey spanned some three years of my getting to know Ricardo. I don't know his whole story, or how he got on the streets. But I see his deep chocolate eyes, and his purposed steps, as he walks with his backpack over his shoulder.

And I know we are friends, so I asked him, "So how are you? Do you need any batteries for your radio?"

With a stammer, he replied, "No, my batteries are good, but, someone stole my sleeping bag."

I piped in with, "I can get you one."

"Really? A used one ... will do just fine. I just need an old one."

"I don't have a used one. I'll need to get you a new one."

"No, I don't need ... new. Old is good."

"But I don't have an old one at the house. So it's new ... or nothing."

He grinned. "I hate for you to get a new one."

"I love new things. I expect you do, too."

He wiped his brow and his words stuttered with vowels wrapped around several letters at a time, and he sighed, a breath of hope. "I'm not sure why someone took my old one."

I slapped his shoulder with a Pam-joy slug. "I do. It's so you can get a new one."

"Thank you. I can't believe I'm getting a new one."

"I can. It's nothing but the best for a friend."

He embraced me with a shaky arm. "Thank you. I can't believe this."

At the store, I had two choices. Blue or yellow, so I got the blue one. The yellow was a wee bit bright even for me. Blue was better.

I share these stories with you because I love how God brings this all together. For you see, this was one of several items for friends on that delivery: a new backpack, new tennis shoes, and yes, some McDonald gift cards for another certain friend at The Bridge.

The best part of that day was that the Lord sent a friend to my office the day prior and he dropped a wad of money on my desk. He wanted to touch the life of some of my homeless friends with kindness, and this is not the first time either

Those moments make my heart swell with joy because I love how God prepares the way; I simply tote, talk, and teach—and go shopping for the Lord.

There are so many silent "givers" in Bowie County who touch the lives of others, and I couldn't do what I do without all of those who love like Christ.

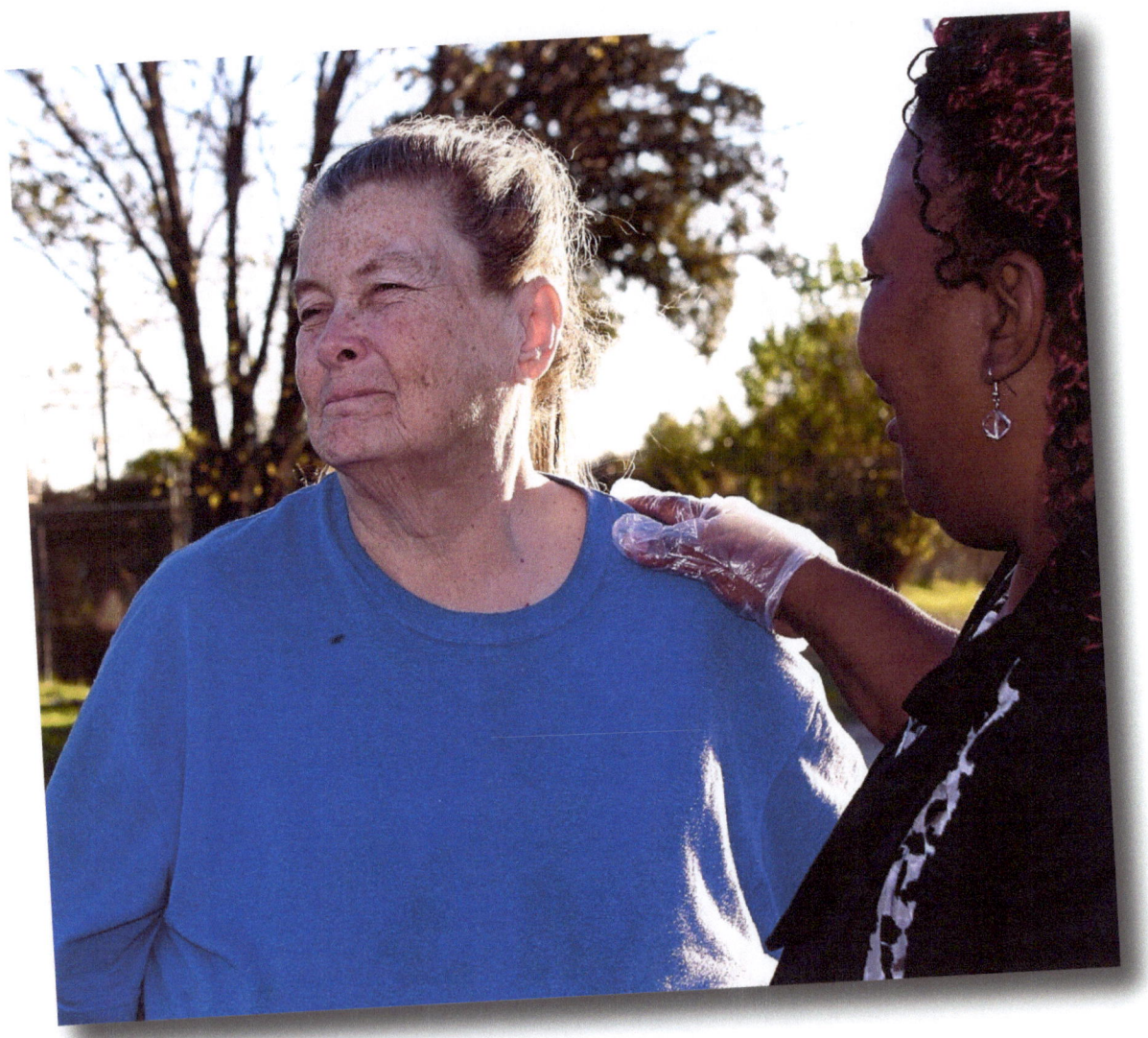

Have Toys! Have Crackers! Will Travel!

I enjoy hitting the streets of Texarkana and loving on the homeless, not just at The Bridge services on Saturday, but on a weeknight where friendships are made—where I pray and share Christ with others.

So last Wednesday, I passed out juice drinks and peanut butter crackers (more than a hundred, thanks to a donation) and each baggie had a toy inside. And yes, the toys were a hit as well.

The big people (grownups) on the street loved receiving little toys. I suppose it was like getting a Cracker Jacks toy without the caramel popcorn.

That night there were tons of kids and folks outside the Salvation Army due to the cooler weather, and divine meetings to pray and enjoy each other's company unfolded like leaves falling from branches in the autumn air.

One teen boy was a Jesus rapper and another wanted prayer to help him listen to God. Others laughed as they sat on the ledge, and they shared their pursuits, longings, and hopes with me.

One man flipping through the pages of his Bible told me I couldn't pray for him, which surprised me since he was holding such a book in his hands. Hey, don't tell him, but I prayed silently for him anyway.

Many recipients hugged me like it was their first hug in months, while some watched my crazy and hyper ways, like they were assessing whether or not I had a brain under my blonde hair.

Eventually, this one girl, a barely grown young lady asked, "So what are you doing here with us? I don't know you."

I smiled as I gave her a bag of crackers and juice. "I don't know you either. But I need to be with some friends."

"So we're your friends?"

"Sure. I love meeting new people."

She cocked her head to one side, and stared at me. "So are you going to ask me my name?" She didn't wait for an answer and continued her quizzing, while peeking inside her baggie. "Who just passes out snacks from their car?"

"Me, I guess. I tend to tote for God. So who are you?"

"I'm Katy. I need new friends for sure."

The next minutes, we talked about her struggle to make the right choices and her desire to do something meaningful. She was tired of wandering and worrying.

She offered up her next question. "So why are you really doing this?"

"Me?"

"Yeah. You."

"I guess you could say that I love the Lord with all my heart, soul, mind and strength. I love sharing about Jesus."

"No, really?"

A voice from nearby, a friend listening in, yelled from his bike. "That's what she does. She loves God. But we all know she doesn't have a mind. She's kind of crazy."

I yelled back, "Yes. Crazy for Jesus. And I do have a small mind."

The new friend laughed and squealed. "I have a toy ring in my bag. It's blue. I love it."

The rest of the night was filled with more quizzes and more hugs and plenty of good old fashioned laughter. And yes, my cooler of Popsicles was eaten up, too.

A woman staying at the Salvation Army, who loves the banana flavored Popsicles told me, "Ms. Pam, I'm moving into my apartment pretty soon. Isn't that great?"

"Yes. I bet you can't wait."

"I'm being patient because God is guiding me and He has been with me all summer. I even have a job now, and I've never had so many Popsicles in my life either."

I'd met her earlier in the summer when Popsicles were a hit with everyone. The outing was a victory in Jesus sort of night and I love my friends, and love making new ones, too. And who knew, that so many grownups would love having toys inside their goodies, like a toy ring, or a bracelet, or a necklace either.

So, I have one question for you—who can you bless with your friendship today?

They may not be homeless, but they could be lonely and in need of a hug, or in need of your prayers. Make today count—and count your many blessings. Better yet, be a blessing! It could start with a toy ring, or even a package of crackers!

Real Money

A delivery of cash (an amount that makes a difference in someone's day) was privately given to me to help a family. This mom and her three children were moving into a home (since their own home burned) and the mom now had a battery for her car (thanks to another dear couple of friends who made that happen) and now she can go to work.

I wasn't sure where to find her on that Saturday (the mom), and drove to the Salvation Army to see her, but her car was not in the parking lot. I prayed for the Lord to guide me to her and I left to drop off some clothes for the needy at God's Closet, and at a red light I sat in my little Chevy Cruze at the intersection.

I could have driven up to this light at any time and the miracle of the moment would have not timed out exactly as needed, because to my left waving at me with his window down in the passenger seat of the very car (my friend's car) was her middle son (around 12 years) grinning and yelling at me, and literally going ballistic with his arms flapping.

I sat there, lost in my own little world in the car, not aware of the call of "Pam!" coming two feet to my left outside my window.

Finally, I caught the commotion in the corner of my eye, and rolled my window down. I shouted with joy, "I can't believe it's you. What in the world are you doing? Where are you headed?"

"We're going home!"

I followed them home, toured their new house, the one without a fridge, or couch, or even beds. They were using an ice chest, using lawn chairs, and sleeping on air mattresses, but treasured having a roof over their heads.

The mom showed me room after room, sharing the potential, how paint will improve things, and how scrubbing the kitchen and bathroom had made the house smell of Pine Sol.

Her excitement and zeal was so humbling, so when I handed her the money (the amazing gift), she nearly lost her balance and this same little middle son asked, "Mom, can I touch the money? Is it real?"

She let him run his fingers over the bills, her voice quivering. "Thank you doesn't say what's really in my heart. Your friend who gave you this money has no idea how this will help us."

I received a round of hugs from her other two children, and from her, and her smile will forever remain etched in my mind. I'll never forget that moment.

On that day, it's like Christ sat in the car next me, waving at me, calling me by name. It's like He showed me how He directs my steps, or better yet, how He sends my car to the right spot, at the right time. And how He sends friends along my path who have more money than I do!

I wonder, how many times I've missed God by being lost in my own little world. I pray that I roll down the window of my heart and look for ways to shine for Him, even if the parking lot of life seems empty, or the way seems long—because He's the way, truth, and life for our hearts.

He's the fragrance of hope like Pine Sol to our day! Oh wait, some of you would rather not smell Pine Sol, so His fragrance is like a rose of hope for the rest of you!

Birthday Party on the Corner!

Another story about my friend Ricardo unfolded in October of 2015, when he told me, "In four days it's my birthday. I'll be 65 years old."

For some reason, the idea of his being alone on his birthday really tugged on my heart, so four days later, I ran to the store and loaded up my cart with birthday goodies.

My friend Cindy and I wanted to surprise Ricardo, which took us to the streets in Texarkana, in search of the birthday boy.

He usually sat on certain benches along the street, so I drove up and down them, even getting confused and driving on the wrong side—which made Cindy yell at me. I was so intent on finding Ricardo I was distracted and not focused on my driving.

Finally, as the sun lowered behind the Grim Hotel, I caught a glimpse of Ricardo sitting by himself on a bench next to his backpack.

Parking my car, we hurried to Ricardo, and decorated him in blue crepe paper while pinning a 'birthday-boy' ribbon badge on his shirt, and I handed him a card with a new coat.

We also had a rainbow birthday cake just for him, a miniature one, along with cupcakes for later.

The card held a wee bit of money too, and inside I'd written a note: *Happy Birthday. You are only as old as you feel. I'm not sure how old 65 feels.*

His laugh told me he approved of the party, and the three of us partied like we were all teenagers.

We also had party favors, and we sang to him, teasing him, and telling him that he was a package of hope. Ricardo's favorite gift was his Hot Wheels Batman car, which Cindy insisted I buy.

And of course, he loved the car most of all, saying the toy car was a keeper.

That night was the first time he told me he had two grown sons and he shared their names, and how life unraveled when he got divorced back in 1994. He missed his boys, and said they would have loved the party.

Well for me, this was the best birthday party ever, but also sad. His being alone still tugged on my heart, but for a little while he was not by himself, and his day was filled with music, sweets, gifts, laughter and friends.

You know, life can send us to the bench alone—without loved ones around us. It can break our heart. It can blow out the candle of hope. It can pin our backs against the wall.

So a few minutes of letting someone know they are not forgotten can remind a person to persevere, and to rise again with a new strength found in Christ.

Sure, I know. I have no idea what his entire story is, or what all the broken pieces were that sent him to the streets. But I do know that if for some reason I can remind Ricardo that he is fearfully and wonderfully created, then he might find renewed strength to move from the bench with a fresh start.

So after the party with Ricardo, Cindy and I drove to the Salvation Army and handed out the rest of his party favors to other homeless friends, along with more cupcakes and we all sang "Happy Birthday" to Ricardo again, even though he was three blocks away.

I wanted my friend to know he can face tomorrow, and anyone else for that matter, because Christ lives—and all birthdays matter.

If you have ever been alone on your birthday, may you know God sees you, loves you, and is ready to wrap you in crepe-paper of hope. He may not bring you a Batman Hot Wheels car for your birthday, but He did send His son Jesus just for you. Just for you! And that's the best birthday present ever! Life everlasting through Christ!

Worth Repeating

Several years ago, I began texting someone's son who was on a lost trail of despair. For days upon days, he never answered my texts—until one day he picked up the call.

On that cold December night, I drove to Texarkana, going up and down the streets, only to eventually purchase food for him, hoping for the moment when I would find him.

I figured that he needed food for his physical body, like chicken, and Gatorade and bananas. Everyone needs bananas. After all, if I get cramps in my legs, surely he might, too.

And yet, I sat in my car in a parking lot waiting for the next directions on my phone, as the first two hours had left me confused, and the night was filled with twists and turns that did not lead me to my friend.

He talked of suicide earlier, so I knew his life was in a fragile place. I had to find my friend's son before it was too late.

Then, it happened, my phone lit up. I was back on the road, driving, turning, and watching the shadows in the night, hoping and praying, and watching and weeping for this young man's lost soul. I so wanted to find him.

His journey of broken choices, his steps of sadness were all coming together and landing on the curb in front of a school in the late evening when most were putting on pajamas. He had finally given me good directions.

I'd made a call to Pastor Cody, who happened (thankfully by God's directing his steps) to be in town and only a few blocks away. He drove to the location with me, to make sure all was well, and that I was safe, but also so we could help our friend get off the streets.

Before the night was over, my wandering friend's son would be situated in a homeless camp. Between Cody and me, we had a tent, blankets, a coat, and even a pillow.

For a short while, my friend would stay at the camp, come to The Bridge for services, only to then get arrested. I'd go see him in jail and see his tears, and hear his cry of wanting to change, of being utterly broken.

He would serve time, and while in prison down the highway, my friend surrendered his life and his heart in obedience to the call of Christ. The Savior gave my friend a new heart, with new desires, and with hope. He accepted the mercy of Christ and started renewing his mind.

Some of his relationships were wounded. Some seemingly beyond repair. But with Christ, I never want to forget that we serve a restoring and redeeming Savior. He can move mountains and fill in those canyons of lost chapters.

Now, it's years later, and after holding a job and working in a town not too far away, and with loving the Lord, serving Him, and regularly studying and worshiping God in a church setting, and surrounding himself with other followers in Christ, and taking new steps of faith—my friend was reunited with his three children. This part of his life was a broken place that seemed severed into pieces. Only God made a way, or could have restored such a broken chapter.

I don't always see the end of the story or the life-change in people whom I meet and love on for Christ, but there's layers to this story that would take hours to unfold if I told you how the Lord also allowed me to minister to his ex-wife at the same time, in a different way.

Yes, Christ called my wandering friend to a new life in Him. He was adopted, chosen, and saved through faith in Christ.

I think back to when my friend first got arrested after he was staying at the camp and how he had left behind his Bible, and how someone found it at his camp and got it to me.

I made sure it got back to him in jail, but before I did, I found myself flipping through the pages of his Bible. In 1 Corinthians 13, my friend had written the date of the night when I had found him on the side of the road. It was scribbled in the margin.

I believe the Lord let me see how much of an impact we can make by showing His love for others. When my friend felt utterly alone and filled with despair, God sent me. I hold no answers, but I do know Christ who is/was the answer. For we are to share the Gospel. Now if the Lord can send me, He can send you to love on others for Christ, too.

That verse in the Bible next to his notes read: Love bears all things, believes all things, hopes all things, and endures all things.

Bibles, Blessings and Plenty of Love

I opened my big mouth and boldly announced to a friend in Dallas that I'd help her get Bibles for her homeless ministry. And oddly enough, I'd never even met this friend—in real life, only on Facebook. And I only had one small problem. I didn't have any Bibles.

Not long after my saying I'd bring Bibles to her, someone brought me some cash just in case I knew of a need. Then a man slipped some folded bills into my pocket right before I shared a Bible story at an event later in the day.

Then, the next day that man's wife brought me a sealed envelope with several large bills. She didn't know her husband had given me some money first, and while I was at lunch at work, another woman brought an envelope with cash. Each donation was given with the idea to meet needs for people God put in my path.

So a handful of people donated money to me within 24 hours which allowed me to do more than just take Bibles to Carolyn. I picked up several Bibles from a mission in Atlanta, and then bought fifty at the Texarkana Lifeway Christian Store. The amount I saved on the portion of Bibles I purchased allowed me to buy 100 socks in Dallas.

I'd leave town for my three-hour drive with nearly 100 Bibles, with 360 protein bars (thanks to another donation), and also with a hundred or more donated brand new shirts that hadn't sold at a store.

Then, get this, the precious folks who were loving on the homeless, Carolyn Hale and Diana Hightower, were praying about how to feed their friends for Thanksgiving, and the rest of the money in my possession ... yes, the rest was given to them. They were able to prepare a meal for dozens and dozens and dozens of their folks under The Bridge who lived in the tent community.

On my trip to Dallas that weekend, even my jacket landed on the shoulders of Thurman who was wrapped in a blanket. I met Rosemary, who's blind and who let me pray for her husband in prison and she wept and praised God.

Robert loved his Bible. Temesha wept when we prayed for her. One man quizzed me about God, and we discussed certain scriptures. Now, I didn't know all the verses, but this man did—and he loved giving me a test.

Other people gently touched the covers of their new Bibles, and hot dogs were consumed on our outing that day. Drinks, too. And love was shared, tears shed. But laughter abounded, and prayers went up.

Late in the afternoon, a precious young woman wandered by for food and before she knew it, she received the love of Christ into her heart, and surrendered her walk and life to the Savior who found her on the street corner. She then wanted to go home, and my friend loaded her into the car along with that new Bible—for a ride home to her little girl and family.

That day was filled with complete joy, and when I got home around midnight, I was exhausted, but smiling. I was also saddened at seeing hundreds living in the tent community, though. But oh, the love and kindness they showed to us, and oh, the humble hearts I met.

One man said, "I'll cry if you pray for me."

I responded, "I'll just have to cry with you then." And I did!

Yes, opening my big mouth sent me on a journey of seeing the mighty hand of God at work! I think I'll have to be bold for the Lord again. Maybe I'll do it today!

Fragrance at The Bridge

One Saturday, a tall, skinny man walked up to me after the service at The Bridge, and he towered over me by a good two feet, and he told me his name.

He checked out my name, too, since someone told him, "Ms. Pam has your shoes."

A few weeks prior, I'd gotten a text about a size-13 shoe for someone, but I had no idea who the man was, only that his feet were in need. And they were big.

Turns out, I've carried his brand new tennis shoes in my trunk for three weeks, but we hadn't connected. I just kept moving the shoes deeper into the trunk until the moment we found each other. "I saved them for you."

He whispered, "So you just kept them?"

"I did. I prayed we'd see each other soon, and you'd get them. They were waiting for your toes. I bought them for you."

Thanking me, his surprise at my having them seemed to overwhelm the young man. He kept saying, "You have my shoes."

He followed me to my car along the small trail by The Bridge, and at the trunk I put them into his hands, and he fell in love with his brand-spanking-new tennis shoes, stroking the leather, holding them close to his chest.

Oh wait, the shoes were probably not leather. They were probably made of rubber, but either way, he loved them.

Two other ladies who were apparently on the day's journey with my lanky friend, lingered, and I pulled some gorgeous neck scarves from a sack in my trunk, those given to me.

I wrapped the end of one scarf around one neck, then the other. The purple, turquoise, and blue colors draped warmth around their necks, and the two ladies nearly twirled with excitement while touching the scarves. Actually, we all twirled, a little that morning.

One of the ladies said, "This smells so good," as she sniffed the fabric, and I leaned in for a whiff, taking in the fragrance, too. I noticed the fragrance was like vanilla, strawberry and caramel all wrapped inside the threads, and we all lingered in the fragrance of just being together, sniffing the scarves.

I waved goodbye as they crossed the road, only to feel compelled to pray with the trio, so I called them back. We met in the middle of the road, and this led to me sharing the fragrance of God's love, and his salvation through Christ on the cross.

Their smiles, my smile, and the warm toes of a new friend sent warmness through my body, from my head to my toes—like a scarf of hope. For me, speaking life to hearts, offering a word of encouragement, and sharing Christ is the best way to spend time, even if it does seem that I find myself in the middle of a road a lot of the time.

So be careful if you drive downtown on Saturday mornings, or on Wednesday nights (street ministry happens after work then), for you may need to dodge me, or those I meet along the way. Or you could simply stop and get out of your car and come pray with us. Besides, I can always use another friend, or someone to direct traffic around our prayer circle.

Disobedient Me

Maybe this will encourage someone that the Lord's mercy is new each day. Once, I stopped at a gas station on my way to The Bridge, and this girl on a bike, wearing a hoodie, peddled up to the store in the rain, and she caught my attention.

Now I have no idea if she was homeless, or without a car and just had to get to work. But I do know, I parked right in front of her and watched her get soaked.

I moved my car from the pump to the front door, and sat in my car wearing not only a gray hoodie, but also my most favorite brown-lined raincoat/coat. I opened the door, and walked by her, going inside, and noticed her dampness even more, and the backpack on her shoulders.

Inside my heart and my mind, I heard these words: give her your raincoat. I totally ignored them, paid for my gas, got into my car and pulled away.

A few blocks away, I then again argued with myself. Or argued with God, and I'd say. "This is my favorite coat. I love this coat. It's huge. Soft. Comfy. It keeps me dry."

I kept driving, only to turn around and go back to that area (which is why I was late to The Bridge) and I hoped to see the girl on her bike. I drove up and down the road in all directions, and pulled through the parking lot of the shopping centers nearby. But I never saw her.

I then went back to the store and asked the clerk if she saw the girl, knew the girl, or if she might know where she worked or lived. Nope. Nothing. No recall. The clerk didn't even remember the girl. And she just stared at me like I was crazy.

Back in my car, I proceeded to tell the Lord how sorry I was for my disobedience, and I totally regretted my selfishness. Yes, I tend to give things away, often, and yes, I give away things that belong to those who ride in my car. And yes, I definitely pass along the things many of you give me, but on this day—I failed the Lord—and I failed this girl.

After The Bridge service, I met someone, and delivered her a black coat that was inside my trunk. Now this was a planned meeting, and I offered her the long-to-the-knees leather coat and yes, my brown-lined-furry-favorite coat, to let her pick from either one. I think I felt guilty from the earlier failure.

She took the black one. It fit her perfectly and the purple and black scarf went with it, too.
While driving home, I talked to the Lord and I lingered in my failure (from earlier) for not listening to God, repenting of it again. Then (don't think I'm crazy), but I knew I'd be ready for the next cold or wet person I saw out in the weather.

I began to weep, "Lord, I'll keep watch. Nothing I have is really mine. It's all yours. I want—I will do better."

Now by the time you're reading this I hope to have given my coat away. I hope to see the smile on someone's face when she's dry and warm. Aren't you thankful for new mercies from God each day? They're like raindrops for the weary heart, like dry socks when you're soaked!

Wrong Way on the Right of Way

The weather dropped fiercely during a service at The Bridge one January. Hands were cold. Faces red. Toes tingled from the chill. My hands, face, and toes felt like they were about to break off, and I ached from the cold as the temperature dropped ten degrees in less than an hour.

Later, inside my car, the heater blew warm air, zapping the cold and warming my skin, and I stopped shaking. My plan included driving the streets in town to love on the homeless, when I saw this man pushing what seemed like his life in a cart down the road.

I inched along, passing him, and remembered I had hand warmers, blankets, gloves, and socks inside my trunk. Now this awesome friend (probably your neighbor) thought she was actually donating them for the homeless ministry in Dallas, but I needed to warm my new cart-friend instead.

I mean, when the weather changed like it did, the abundance in my car became the "abundance of warmth" for many I'd meet that morning. So when I saw the man with the cart, I pulled to the side of the road, opened my trunk and grabbed some items, thinking I'd drive up alongside the man, using wisdom in my approach.

I zipped a U-turn and went down the road where I had watched his wobbly walk push the overloaded cart down the asphalt. He was gone. He must have taken an alley or made a turn, and I'd missed him.

I shook my head at my lack of hurrying, and drove up a block and turned right. There he was off to the right ... the right ... but it was a one-way street to my left. This meant I had to take another street, make some more turns and get myself aligned to meet this man with my goodies.

I did just that, only now, he'd made a turn up the other road, going north which meant I was not driving on his street anymore. I made a turn, a stop, and another turn. Finally, yes, finally, I pulled up and the man who walked to my left and who was headed the opposite way—next to my driver's side window.

I called to him from my open window, "I know you. I know you."

He stepped toward the car, letting go of the cart. "You're the Popsicle lady from this summer. I know you, too." He smiled. "Are you following me? I've seen your car about six times."

I jumped from the car. "Yes, I'm following you. I have some hand warmers. Aren't you freezing?"

"I am. I just left my wife. She's at the Salvation Army."

"Here, take this blanket. And the gloves. And here's several more hand warmers."

His hug around my neck came with, "God bless you. I'm glad you followed me."

"Me, too. Can I pray with you about your needs?"

We'd go on to pray, to chat, and I'd listen (I can, really) and the entire time, my little blue car sat at the stop sign idling ... and not ONE car came our way! Although my friend did have to rescue his cart when it tried to roll away!

I treasure such moments. I treasure Christ. I treasure my friends who love my homeless friends and keep my car packed with items that come in handy at the exact moment when they are needed. That's how God works, as He sends us all out into the world to be messengers of His hope and share His glory, even when it's freezing.

Besides, you never know who is waiting around the bend if you'll drive around the block one more time. You might get a hug in the middle of the road, too. One that warms you like ten blankets! Like hand warmers for your heart!

Songs for the Heart on a Corner

From somewhere in the wind, the wrinkled man appeared like a tall tree in his boots and cowboy hat. The hat was black. The shirt. The pants. And yes, the boots were black, too. Against the reflection from the clouds in the sky, his outfit appeared like the color of deep charcoal.

His unkempt gray beard whipped in the wind like bristles on a broom, and he tapped his foot on the dead grass.

Strumming the smoky-colored guitar with his calloused fingers, I'm sure a tune rose up like blooms on a flower, but no one could hear the song from the rush of the highway cars roaring by on the road.

He stood in the medium between the entrance and exit signs in the road leading to and from the giant retail store. And still, he played, all the while, grinning and singing and swaying.

I sat in my car in the parking lot next to this one-man concert and gathered up the gazillion quarters and dimes and loose change in the middle of my dash (had already depleted my other funds) to give them to him.

So I poured the money into my friend's hands (she was in the passenger seat), and I'm thankful for this brave person (Cindy Ross) who dares to ride with me on ministry outings. It's not like she doesn't already know that I'm not your normal run of the mill friend, let alone street ministry gal.

She gave me her, "You're making me get out of the car and forcing me to love on this man for Christ stare"—stare.

I returned the glare with my, "I know you can do it"—and she finally (reluctantly) stepped from the car, and rushed to the man, carrying the money.

I'm sure she offered him kind words, as I saw them smiling at each other. Turns out, she told him about her own love of music, too. See, they had kindred hearts.

Somehow, I expect those steps across the parking lot for my friend to the man strumming his songs, did something to her heart. As she weathered the cold, she spoke to the stranger on the side of the road, and she allowed God to guide her.

I also expect it made her feel not so alone herself. I know that it made my own heart swell with hope at seeing them interact, at her obedience to loving like Christ.

Now before you think I simply watched, I did chase down my own stranger who walked like a tumble weed in the wind, and I tripped on the curb hurrying to his side. I made friends with the red-faced man wearing the heavy coat, as he limped. He told me he apparently can walk better than I do, and he laughed at me. I handed him some hand-warmers for his exposed hands, too.

So take the "Pam you can do it for God"—challenge and seek out the lonely and let them know Christ loves them! Share the hope of Jesus with them, too. It can be music to your soul! And to theirs! But be ready, there's no telling what God will have you do—if you have eyes to see and ears to hear! Especially if you have a friend like me to push you out of the car!

When Random Becomes Regular

A random stop at a certain spot. A parking space in front of the restaurant in a place I never park. The light brightly shining on the area. A white coat glowing in the shadows across the street. That appeared like a robe draped on the shoulders of a woman. Could it be my friend?

I glanced. I squinted. I wondered. I recognized her. She's a homeless friend who walks the sidewalks, the streets, sits on benches, and walks some more. You'll see her often. Daily. And probably never really see her. Unless you look.

She darts in and around and up and down the streets of Texarkana. On this night the temperatures would drop down into the 30s, and at the moment I saw her, it was already around 45 degrees. Chilly. Cold. Getting colder. Definitely, getting darker.

Now this random stop, or not so random stop of pulling into this parking spot, along with the light; they all brought me to a place where I desired to hold and hug my dear friend, and to also honor the Lord by showing kindness to her. Hugs are something we all long for, if we're honest.

For a brief moment, my robe-coat friend stepped into the road in front of a rushing car. A car that never slowed, never honked. Now the driver might not have seen her, except the WHITE coat did cause a glare even in the shadows.

This SUV seemed to inch closer, rolling ahead in slow motion, and as fast as she moved to the street, my friend's feet gingerly slid to the curb, getting her out of the way.

I rushed inside McDonald's for a minute, and hurried back. She was gone. I drove around the corner, over the bridge and twisted my head in every direction in hopes of finding her. I had lost her to the shadows (something I've done often on the streets), so I decided to drop off clothes at God's Closet because I needed to meet up with someone else who had some pressing needs.

Upon my return, leaving town, I spoke to God: Help me find my robe-friend. You can't miss her coat. She's out there. Help me.

At the red light, the next light, the very next stop, yes, a mere hundred feet ahead, I saw the WHITE coat in a parking lot. I cut across the lanes (yes, I waited for the green light), and my friend turned around with a jolt, stopping in the spotlight of—the hope of the Lord. Or my car!

I jumped from my seat and our hearts were connected in the chill of the night, and she finally received her McDonald's meal. She does love their burgers. And fries! And the soda!

So if you're able, accept the 'white-coat' challenge of the day and love on someone for the Lord! It's worth the drive—but always keep watch, the traffic of distraction will do its best to get in the way. Or run you over. Or cause you to miss the opportunity.

Instead, try this; seek the Lord and ask Him whom you might bless, but do it before the cold of nightfall slips in. And do it better than me. For my ways come with using more gas in my car than I should, and with making lots of U-turns! But thankfully, the Lord orders my steps!

Candy in Church

A dear friend who walks the streets pretty much nonstop asked me, "Ms. Pam, would you mind getting me some Butterfingers?"

I was surprised by the request, but of course said, "Sure. Yes, of course."

Now while I'm at this little retail store, it gets robbed. I had no idea that it happened because I was in the back of the store. I was searching for other items I needed, like instant coffee for Eddie and Tony, and I found tarps that cost $3.50!

I loaded down my arms, and I kept dropping my items, and stacking them back, and all the while, I'm in the rear aisles of the store. Thankfully, I dropped everything more than once, which gave the robbers time to get out of the store without hurting anyone—or me.

Finally, I make it to the front after the incident and I'm like a toddler who wanders in after the excitement and apparently, I'm the only brave person who asks if we can still check out.

I pay for my items, and started looking for my sweet friend to give her the candy, and nearly ran over Eddie and Tony. But they got their coffee though! I couldn't find my Butterfinger friend; I think she gave up on me. I probably took too long.

Hours later, after I've played with my grandson at the park, I headed back to town to listen to a dear friend give her testimony at her church, and I'm sitting in this service during worship, and in walked ... drum roll ... in walked my friend who wanted the candy!

I had kept the three giant packages of Butterfingers in my car just in case I saw her in the next few days, and then she suddenly was sitting across the row from me ... I mean, straight across!

My friend shared her heart, and I wept and rejoiced at listening to her. And at the end of the service, I glanced over and my little homeless friend was gone.

Oh, but wait! Nope!! She wasn't gone! She had moved next to my friend Cindy in our row on the other side of us. She'd joined us at some point, and was sitting two seats over from me, grinning!

So yes, she received her candy! And I was thrilled! Candy at church is always great! It's sweetness for the night and also joy— which is all wrapped in one when you see a friend at church! When she wants to sit with you!! When she smiles!! And when her jaw drops on the ground when she gets the candy you saved for her, too!!

Miss Our Daddy

I miss my dad, especially whenever I finish writing a book, or whenever I embark on a new chapter in life, or long for his voice, or when his birthday comes around. At the publishing of this book, my dad would have been 101, and he passed away in 1998, although it feels like yesterday and yet, like forever.

Well, not long ago, I saw a man, alone, in a parking lot, who stood next to a rundown car. An older guy. Bent somewhat. And he held a sign, which I tried to read as I drove on by, hurrying inside to pick up the items on my list.

As I pulled back down the lane with my sacks in the backseat, he now sat on the edge of the driver's seat with the car door open. His car was parked at an angle to catch the attention of shoppers turning into the parking lot, and the sign sat propped up against the panel next to him, and he rested his head in his hands, slumping forward.

I slowed to read the sign, which had these words: *When you see me, do you see your dad?*

I immediately felt this tug on my heart even though the man looked nothing like my dad, but my longing for my own dad grew intense and brought tears to my eyes. Oddly enough, I'd just had a phone conversation with my mom about my dad, and how he played Santa for some kids when I was three.

We had talked of how he loved to fish and how he was surrounded by the police once while camping. It seems a helicopter landed, and they searched his blue truck at the lake in Arizona. Not that he was wanted, they had the wrong man. Nothing bothered my dad, and he finished eating his breakfast during their search.

Another time, my dad was walking across a field carrying his shotgun in Coffeeville, Texas. My grandma said to us (my twin and I, we were little), "There comes your daddy."

My sister ran to the window and said, "I don't see that baby's daddy."

My mom called us 'baby' since she wasn't always sure which twin to scold, or who was getting in trouble.

So when I saw the man by the car, I thought of my dad and the memories flooded through my mind. I began to cry, and I parked my car over a few lanes, assessing the surroundings. I wasn't sure what that would include, but I watched the man who might be someone's father, and I wiped tears from my face. All I could hear in my head was this, *I SEE that baby's daddy. And he needs help.*

So yes, his name is Jerry. I did meet him, and prayed with him, too. I also discovered a few tidbits about him, and learned he's a follower of Christ. He's hit hard times. Ran out of money. And wanted to get home.

As I drove off, he waved in the dark, clutching the money I'd given him, and tossed the sign in the back seat and went straight to the gas pumps.

How do I know this? Because I too, was on empty and ended up pulling up next to him at the gas station. He hollered from the other spot at the pumps, "Hey, don't I know you?"

I yelled back, over the roar of the rushing traffic. "You sure do. I'm your new friend."

He called back, "You're a good one. Thanks for the gas. You look like my daughter, a little bit. Although she's got brown hair. And she's smaller."

I shook my head. "Then I don't think we favor. I'm blonde. And I'm not so little."

"Oh, but you do favor. She's got the best smile ever. Just like you."

And that's when I nearly pumped gasoline all over my car!

For a short time, it was like I stood at the window and I could remember my dad's blue eyes, and his smile, and it was like I could see him coming across the field! Almost! Almost!

The Gospel at Starbucks

At The Bridge that spring Saturday, I was challenged to share the Gospel after hearing Pastor Cody's teaching. So later as I stepped in line around noon to purchase a 'caffeine fix' at Starbucks, I found myself thinking on his message and also standing—at the wrong end of the aisle.

A tall, weathered, lanky man made eye contact with me, and he told me, "Ladies first."

I nodded, ordered my drink, and then lingered to pay for his.

He ordered a small coffee, and I interrupted him, "Get what you want. I've got this."

The man smiled, "Make that a large coffee. That would be great."

As I scanned the app on my phone to pay for our coffee, he turned to me. "Do you know Jesus?" And he handed me a Gospel tract.

Of course, I woke everyone up inside Starbucks by shouting, "Yes. I know Jesus."

We talked outside and I shared with him how I was going to witness to him, but he beat me to it.

He wiped a tear, "I'm just a hobo (his word) and I serve Christ. I share the Gospel."

Now some of you know I write the novel series, *Annie Grace Kree Chronicles* about a hobo girl who rides the rail. So needless to say my heart was taken by Wallace's story.

We hugged, we laughed, and he told me a story of being converted in a parking lot years back. Of serving time in prison. He shared some broken chapters, but shared the redemption of Christ, too.

By now, I'm sitting across from my new friend, but Wallace CAN share Christ and be bold, it's a moment that left me quite humbled. For we all need truth. We all need the love of Christ.

I was blessed beyond any caffeine fix by hanging out with my new friend, and I'll treasure the tract he gave me—forever.

If any of you would like me to share Jesus with you, I'd be more than happy to share the good news with you. And maybe we could do it over a cup of coffee!

Later in the year, Wallace came up missing and I prayed for his safety, along with others. Weeks went by, but eventually we heard good news—his family heard from Wallace, he simply took a road trip without telling anyone.

And I'm sure, if he stayed true to character, Wallace shared his Gospel tracts with others along the way!

Josh, My Friend

I have a passion for being on the streets to love on someone for the Lord. And in March of 2016, a friend of mine was stabbed across the street from the Salvation Army. When I heard of his death, I was undone, and felt horrible. I felt like I failed him spiritually—not sure, not knowing if my friend, Josh, was saved. If he was a follower of Christ.

Sure, I'd been on the street that same week, and watched two of my homeless friends drag cardboard boxes down the street like they were carrying paneling fit for a king. Their smiles had welcomed me to their unshaped cardboard-castle world.

I happened to have a couple of bedding pads (plastic ones made out of hundreds of little white trash bags). And the two men gazed at the pads like they were holding million-dollar padding to sleep on.

Then on the same night, another homeless friend came out of the Salvation Army after taking a shower. I was handing out goodies when she saw a small sack in my trunk, "What's in here, Ms. Pam?"

"That's just some old-lady shoes. You don't want them."

I ripped into the bag anyway. They were her size, and they were NOT old-lady shoes, but brown ankle-type Ropers and they were nice, and perfect, just for her.

Her laughter rang out like joy escaping from a deep well where lost giggles and hope get trapped.

Minutes later, she shared in a whisper how a friend got arrested, and about her hopes for him, for them, and she asked me to pray. Her smile ran deep into the crevices of her face where trouble hides, where broken steps stay.

She bellowed out her goodbye after our prayer. "I think these shoes are awesome. And they are made for YOUNG people, not old, Ms. Pam."

It was another great outing to love on my friends!

So when my friend, Josh woke up for the last time a few days later, and when he attended Church Under the Bridge, and heard the Gospel for the last time—I was reminded how he came to my assistance the week before when another bridge friend was a little aggressive toward me. Now it's not all pretty on the street, nor in our churches either, and this 'stressed-out' friend blocked my car door, keeping me from getting inside.

Josh made sure I was safe, even putting himself between me and the other person for a moment. He talked quietly and calmly to disarm the situation, and the not-so-happy friend went on down the road. God used Josh to save me. God sent him my way, I'm sure of it.

But If I'd known someone was going to stab Josh, and kill him, I would have more passionately shared salvation in Christ with him.

Pastor Cody said, "I cannot satisfy the heart of any man, but I can lovingly point them to the Christ, who can. So strive every day to live passionately, live purposefully, throw your life away in service to others, redeem the time and wield the mighty power of the Gospel in your daily life, trusting in God to mightily save."

And so, I agree with Pastor Cody, "Let's go and tell—lives matter, time is short, and Jesus saves!"

I Met Wonder Woman

I did it! I saw my first 3-D movie at the theater in 2016. Now it wasn't a movie you'd normally see me buying a ticket for: well, actually I didn't even buy the ticket.

And seeing me sit with my feet on the rail like a teenager isn't something you could call as normal either. But everyone else did it, so I followed suit.

Wearing those glasses made me feel carsick though, but it's like I was actually flying with Superman and riding in Batman's car. So I didn't mind too much.

Yes, that's right. I went to the new *Batman Vs Superman* movie, but let me tell you how it unfolded and why I think God sovereignly used this movie to draw me in.

Earlier that night, I had gotten a text from Pastor Cody with words telling me he was picking up some of our friends from the homeless camps for dinner.

I was committed to a task right after work, thus, my response was a no—I couldn't go. However, about an hour later, my phone buzzed again, and another text came with an invite to join them at the movie.

Seems Pastor Cody took the men back to the camps, but he and his little boy were taking Nora to the movie, to a movie Cody's son wanted to see—a superhero movie with plenty of action.

I'd learn that while everyone ate at the restaurant this little tyke kept asking to go to a show, and everyone pretty much ignored him except for Nora—who said she'd like to see this movie.

That's how I ended up going with them. How I wore the glasses. How I screamed at the objects flying at my face (seemingly). How I sat next to Nora.

How I laughed like a toddler. How I learned more about Nora, too. How I got in trouble for talking during the show. How I discovered Nora's love for fast-paced action movies.

How she loved Superman as a child. How Batman is the guy with the cool car. How Lex Luther is an evil super villain. How I love Clark Kent's hair.

But by now, you're asking me how this movie outing is a sovereign move of God?

Well, the next morning at The Bridge service (for the homeless), Nora approached me, holding her Bible, telling me she wanted to go through a Bible study with me, to learn more of what is inside the pages.

By the time you are reading this I will have met Nora at the library for months—and we will have studied our Bibles together. We will have sat together. Searched for meaning. Scoured the verses. And moved closer as friends.

And to think, a trip to a movie where dizzy and fun unfolded—allowed me to get closer to *Wonder Woman*—and I'm talking about Nora, not the character in the movie. Nora is amazing, full of life, and filled with hope for her future. Her sense of humor is contagious.

Besides, I've learned something else—all of us have the potential to become a superhero for the Lord. We can fly into the day with hope like Superman, or drive like Batman to meet a friend with kindness, or wield our faith to encourage someone, too.

We are to be lights for Christ in a world that's too busy, often brash, and certainly bogged down—for on certain days sitting next to someone at the movie is the best way to shine a light into a dark room like a flashlight of hope when things can seem bleak.

So if you need some 3-D glasses, I have some special specs. They allow you to see into a heart—well, at least they did when a homeless friend grabbed my heart and trusted me with hers.

And that doesn't make me dizzy or carsick at all! It gives me a reason to trust God more—for He uses us when we least expect it, when we're anything but *Wonder Woman*!

S'mores for No One

I had gone to the Dollar Store to meet a need for one of my friends when I found myself buying two bags of marshmallows, three giant Hershey bars, and two boxes of graham crackers in hopes of sharing them with someone, who might need to have a spring party.

I jogged over to some friends at the park with my sacks, and one of them ran to me, thinking something was wrong. My swift moves must have come as a shock, and I assured him I was there to hang out with them.

We stood at the park, laughing, cutting up and talking about the morning church service, about choices and God. And talked about life in general.

One friend used my phone to make a long distance call and he talked forever like a lost puppy who found his family. He's been writing letters to family members, and had gotten a number.

Then a guy I had never met came up on his bike, and he joined our corner-party. I saw another camp-friend, and waved to her and she came over. Then another woman came, and she thought we were acting silly, but she joined us anyway.

There were seven of us now, and we decided we were REALLY having a party and it wasn't even noon. Anyone driving by would have thought children were let loose at the park. We did act like toddlers, or I did. (Ha.)

I told them we could have S'mores, which is what I had hoped they would do with my goodies, fun chocolate-smacking-sugar-rush stuff, that all friends should enjoy at some point.

I learned that Thomas didn't like them, but had one when he was a kid. Eddie said he liked his marshmallows to be brown from the fire, but he's not fond of them either. The guy on the bike said, "No, thank you," and Mike pretty much snarled at me.

In other words, no one seemed to be a fan of S'mores and Eddie said, "I think your party is falling apart at the seams."

I asked all of them, "Who likes graham crackers?"

Together they yelled, "We do."

I asked, "Who can tolerate a marshmallow?"

Again, they agreed, they could.

So I asked one more question, "So do you guys like chocolate?"

Their smiles and nods were an obvious, "Yes! Yes!"

I was quick to remind them, "Then we can party without adding the three together. We don't have to mix them, melt them or even stack them. We can SIMPLY eat them."

By the time I left the corner, I'd had the best time—and partied with some amazing friends, and they even kept the items for the S'mores, even if they only ate the goodies one by one—later.

Goodness, I expect God would love a S'more. Now, I have to confess, I don't like S'mores either. I think I got drawn in by the commercials I've seen on TV! They make them look so good!

Well, they did make for a great topic with friends at the park—for sure

Angel Wings

A run to town after work for street ministry offered amazing encounters that night. For I met Greg who was sitting on some steps and I circled back to park on the corner, to grab a Gatorade, and to get out and meet him.

(Turns out he's staying at the shelter.)

"Hi, I'm Pam. It's hot out here."

"Sure is. Very."

"Looks like I have something you might like."

Greg smiled, and his gold caps sparkled in the sunlight against his brown skin. Shaking my hand, he said, "Thank you. I am thirsty." He took a drink, more like a gulp, and smiled again. "I've been hanging on, thanks to the grace of God. I start my job tomorrow. But you ... you are an angel."

Laughing, I responded, "I've never been anyone's angel before. I'm just Pam who wants to tell you about Christ. That's why I taped a verse on your bottle."

He turned the plastic thirst quencher sideways, "Well, that's a great scripture, and yes, I am 'saved by grace' which is a gift from Jesus for sure."

His friend Tim came up, and I'd seen this man earlier, but his pace on the side of the street was frantic, and kind of erratic so it kept me from driving up to him. But now, he was talking to Greg and me, and Greg told him "Angel Pam is here."

Shaking my head, and giggling a little erratically myself, I handed Tim a Gatorade and his 32 ounces went down before I could blink. I went back to my car for two more bottles and handed them seconds. Tim asked me, "So what is this on the bottle?"

Smiling, I said, "It's one my favorite verses. Ephesians 2:8." I sort of waved at him with a gesture. "To drink the second bottle you have to read it," which he promptly did.

Then I recited the verse, "For by grace you have been saved through faith. And this is not your own doing; it is the gift of God."

Earlier in the evening, I prayed with three ladies, and a man named Brad, and they were surprised I'd stop right there in the field to pray with them. Brad smelled of a drink from another kind of bottle, but he joined us and was attentive.

I held his hands with both of mine, and I told him how he was fearfully and wonderfully made in God's image and that I pray his soul comes to know Jesus, and he stared right through me. But I know Christ redeems, and I'm praying for Brad—that grace and mercy will call to his heart from Christ.

Then I saw Jack sitting on a wall alone. I pulled to the side of the road, and I hopped out, discovering he'd buried his mom, and his sadness required a hug and a prayer. He was so humble. He held my hand. "Thank you for stopping. I don't feel so alone."

I met a girl pushing a stroller, and she was headed to the jail to visit someone, so we talked for a minute, and she even told me she planned to share Jesus with her friend once she got there.

I ran into a family who are moving out of the Salvation Army, and the joy on this mother's face lit up the shadows of her long year—for they have been in the shelter with the children for months.

Before the night ended, twenty-two precious people graced me with their friendship, not counting a dozen children who played across from the Salvation Army. Talking with many about Christ. Listening to them. Hugging them. Praying with them. It was like being in God's presence and with family.

One lady said after I'd prayed, "I could sense God was with us during our prayer, and you just happened to stop here."

I smiled. "I'm sure the Lord had something to do with it," and she agreed.

So three hours on the street left me filled to the brim with joy and hope in Christ. And to think, I finally got my angel wings. Or not!

Medicine for my Heart

Special encounters make my heart soar and make my smile grow wider than a four-lane highway. And that's a pretty big smile! And it begins with my amazing friends!

When a homeless friend waves to me, I love it. When another one smiles, I do, too. When another one prays for me after service, I weep. When another one interrupts another one, and another one interrupts another one, when they are all trying to talk to me, I wish to become a triplet. After all, I am a twin.

It's those moments, special ones—under The Bridge when I am most at home. I could stay for days and months and years. I could linger and lounge, for I love their company.

When a homeless friend pulls my hair like we're little kids. When a friend hugs my neck. When another one calls to me from afar, and I walk up to him, and he says I couldn't get close to you for a hug this morning—all the people were in my way. I then hug him, and we laugh. We also pray. And again, I'm home.

Then another man and woman linger whom I don't know, but he and his family remain with me, nearby, until no one is left and I meet his family, a wife, and three girls. I pray for them, learn a little about their story, and discover they're staying at the Salvation Army.

And then ... I see his face and how it's swollen up like the size of a baseball. He has an infection in his jaw, and has two prescriptions. I take the two papers to go the pharmacy, along with the third prescription for his daughter who has a rash.

Before I go into the pharmacy, I pray, "Lord, you know my budget. You know this family and their dire need. Please Lord, make a way."

I entered the pharmacy, where I shared my heart and my tears (I get emotional when needs are serious because I care). And I knew my budget and it was a wee bit low—and once inside, I discover a kind-hearted pharmacist and his staff.

A wonderful moment unfolded, and the bill ... drum roll ... the bill was NOT much at all, a mere few dollars. You would be shocked at how small!

Not long after that weekend, I ran into this family during the week—no rash, and no swollen jaw! And yes, they're my dear friends now! And so is the pharmacist who blessed this family beyond measure! Blessings I'd miss by not being with my family! Blessings for my heart!

The Little Blue Truck That Could

One night I watched a man hovering under the hood of a not-so-new truck, and caught myself glued to him. I also caught myself knowing, and caught myself retrieving money from the car, too. And I walked to the spot on the rocked-wall where he now chatted with a friend across from the Salvation Army. I interrupted their conversation. "So what's wrong with your truck?"

He glanced up at me. "It's broken down." He used truck-engine talk, as if I understood, and I nodded, and he explained, "It's not the distributor but a piece next to it."

(Yes, he said what it was, but I don't recall the name, as I'd glazed over by then, but I nodded as if I knew all about car parts and engines.)

I quizzed him more, "So how much will this cost? And what's your name?"

"I'm Billy, and maybe $30, or a bit more will fix it. I'm not sure." His words fell silent, his eyes downcast, his pockets obviously empty.

I reached inside my pocket. "I believe the Lord wants to fix your truck."

"Really? You think so?"

I handed him the money. "Yes, and this will get you what you need."

"Are you sure? I don't want to take your money."

"It's not my money. It belongs to God. He simply let me bring it to you."

His face found a smile hidden behind the worry. "I can't believe you have the amount I need."

"I can. We serve a God who cares about you. Billy, can I pray for you?"

"Sure."

I spoke to our mutual friend. "Junior, do you want to pray with us, too?"

Junior hurried to my side and sat on the ledge. "Yes, you know I want to pray. Will you pray for my auntie? She's 85."

I took their hands, "Sure. I can do just that."

Junior sighed, "She's the only auntie I have left."

We prayed together, talked some more, hugged, and said our goodbyes. I moved along to chat with others, to pass out hygiene bags. And then about an hour later, I drove down the highway past an auto parts store.

There was Billy, coming from inside the store carrying a bag in his hand. I figured he had the part to his truck. His gait was strong, and his smile was plastered on his face, and it was like watching "renewed hope" walking down the sidewalk.

By the way, Billy came to church at The Bridge the next weekend and he told me how he'd prayed for a way to fix his car, on the very day I'd met him.

However, after I left, he told me that he'd nearly spent the money on tobacco and cigarettes, but remembered how I had told him the money belonged to God. So he ended up buying the part for his car instead, and now the truck runs. It was like the little-engine-that-couldn't, now could, and like Billy was so excited that he did the right thing—by buying the part for his truck! I'm sure the Lord smiled down upon him, too!!

Royalty at the Concert

I drove across the bridge, turned on my flashers, and put my car in PARK on the side of the road. Since I'd stopped in the right lane and there's no shoulder, I needed to hurry, so I hopped from the driver's seat and rushed to the edge of the bridge.

Hollering, I cupped my hands around my mouth and shouted into the trees below, calling to my homeless friends. "Nora! Nora, are you there?"

From somewhere in the dark, a voice called back. "Is that you, Pam?"

I responded, "Yes, it's me. Hurry, come up the hill. Come here."

Nora appeared from within the bushes and made her way up the concrete hill. "What are you doing here?"

Smiling, I waved my arms. "I have a surprise."

To my left, Randy and Tony joined us, as did Steve, and they all wanted to know what in the world I was doing. Which is a pretty common question.

It was sunset, the shadows were low, and they hadn't expected to hear me shouting at them from the top of the highway on the bridge. But the 'surprise' hadn't come my way in time to come to them in the daylight.

During the day, I don't mind walking their trail, but at night—well, too many snakes for me to meet up with, so that keeps me from strolling in the shadows—thus, the stop on top of the bridge.

I shared my excitement with them. "I won four tickets to the Perot Theater. And I already have my ticket, Cindy and I do, that is."

Now Nora smiled. "Tickets for what?"

"For a concert at the Perot. The band is Big Daddy Weave, also Plumb, and We Are Messengers will perform, and they're playing there this Friday night. And I need to give those tickets to you guys, so you can enjoy the evening listening to them."

Nora's grin grew wider. "Come on guys. This would be fun. It would break our boredom."

Randy asked," What's a Big Daddy Weave?"

"It's a band, You'll like them. They're good, too. And they play Christian songs. You might even like a few of their songs."

The four friends discussed it among themselves on the side of the hill, tossing the idea around, and two of them agreed to come. Nora said yes, and Steve agreed to come.

At that moment, I wasn't sure about Randy and Tony, but I told Nora to find two others if they couldn't come, and to meet me at the Perot at 6 p.m. Friday.

I ran back to my car, waving at my friends as they climbed down the hill. I drove into the sunset, and yes, my smile lit up the car like flashers on a bumper! Like hope in the night. Like a song being played at a concert!

Update: At the concert, Nora sat by me, since my friend Cindy got sick, which worked out perfectly, because we needed her ticket.

See, Randy came. Tony, too. Steve was a no show, but Terry came. And we met a new guy, Ryan, who was so excited to be at the concert—he danced to the songs most of the night praising God with his hands lifted high. His zeal was like a small child who was thrilled to be in the audience!

The night blessed me beyond measure, and dropping off my friends on the top of a bridge around 10:30 p.m., was like dropping off royalty—because their friendship is priceless. And oh, so beautiful!

Boots Sent from Prison to a Homeless Man

One night, my husband delivered some new cowboy boots to me with a message—I was to pass them along to a homeless friend. Now the boots were handcrafted by an inmate, a man, who once lived in my hometown. Somehow he knew I was a part of serving in ministry with the homeless, and sent them my way, assigning me the job of delivering the boots.

Well the following Sunday, I drove around for nearly 45 minutes, going up and down the streets in downtown Texarkana. I couldn't make a decision, and those I saw on the sidewalks weren't wearing boots—so not one of them drew me in, or made me want to stop my car.

I wasn't sure if I was supposed to give the boots away on that morning since time ticked faster than I could keep up. Maybe I was supposed to make a delivery later during the week. But thankfully, the Lord only needs a split second to make "the direction" of what to do perfectly clear to me.

I stopped my car at a corner and asked the Lord to show me "who" or send me home. I wanted to surrender the "me" in the journey and I desired to honor God with my steps and my driving. Thus, I needed to get out of the way and listen to Him.

I inched ahead, and the next thing … the very next thing. I mean, the very next person who came into view, some 20 feet ahead of me, stood with his back to me, and his boots caught my attention.

Driving slower than I should, I stared at the man's feet, waving at him, and I couldn't help but wonder what size shoe he wore. Since I was blocking a car from turning by now, I rushed around the corner and drove back to the street, parking across from the man.

I leapt from my car. "What size shoe do you wear?"

He glanced at his feet. "I wear a 9 1/2 or 10. It just depends."

I explained the story of the boots and how they were made just for him, and how they arrived from a prisoner in a Texas prison. And how they were handcrafted, too.

He asked, "Do you think God sent these boots to me?"

I paused, "What do you think?"

Grinning, he responded, "Well, I was just standing here, and the soles on these old boots are nearly worn through. So it must be God."

I nodded, "Then they are from God. I'm sure of it."

Later, I replayed in my mind how he wasn't standing on the corner when I drove by the first ten times, and how he stroked the leather on the boots. How he hugged them, too. He so loved the boots!

Through tears, I thanked God for allowing me to be a part of such a moment. I also thanked the Lord for using an inmate hours away whom I've never met, to change someone's day, which changed mine. And somehow, I expect the new boots felt like hope for a lonely soul! Or would that be comfort for a worn out sole?

Annie Grace Kree Chronicles Series

1 Untied Shoelace
2 Unknown Soul
3 Rescue of Undaunted Spirit
4 Unwanted Sidekick
#5 Coming 2017
#6 Coming 2018

Other Books by Pam Kumpe

See You in the Funny Papers
A Scoop of Inspiration
Things I Learned in Jail
In the Lick of Time
My View from the Bridge
A Goat with a Tote

www.pamkumpe.com

Leave comments on my Facebook page.
I'd love to hear from you!

www.ingramcontent.com/pod-product-compliance
Lightning Source LLC
Chambersburg PA
CBHW041700160426
43191CB00002B/38